*The Walking Testimony*

# THE WALKING
# TESTIMONY

*My story of tribulations, forgiveness, and victory*

**BRENAJI MARSHAE BROWN**

*The Walking Testimony.*
Copyright © 2021 by Brenaji Marshae Brown.

All rights reserved. No part of this book may be reproduced in any form or by any electronic or mechanical means, including information storage and retrieval systems, without permission in writing from the publisher and author, except by reviewers, who may quote brief passages in a review.

This publication contains the opinions and ideas of its author. It is intended to provide helpful and informative material on the subjects addressed in the publication. The authors and publisher specifically disclaim all responsibility for any liability, loss, or risk, personal or otherwise, which is incurred as a consequence, directly or indirectly, of the use and application of any of the contents of this book.

Certain stock imagery © Shutterstock.com.

ISBN:  978-1-63950-102-1   [Paperback Edition]
       978-1-63950-103-8   [eBook Edition]

Printed and bound in The United States of America.

Gateway Towards Success

1309 Coffeen Avenue
STE 1200, Sheridan,
Wyoming, 82801 USA

+13179780258
*www.writersapex.com*

Scripture quotations marked NIV are taken from the Holy Bible, New International Version®. NIV®. Copyright © 1973, 1978, 1984 by International Bible Society. Used by permission of Zondervan. All rights reserved.

# Contents

Acknowledgments ..................................................................... vii
Introduction ............................................................................ viii

Welcome to My Life .................................................................. 1
Cali Start School ....................................................................... 3
Cali Elementary School ............................................................. 5
Fourth Grade ............................................................................ 8
The Repeat of Fourth Grade ................................................... 11
Heading to Cali Middle School ............................................... 18
Sixth Grade ............................................................................. 23
She Left Me ............................................................................. 27
Cali Junior High ...................................................................... 30
The Bully That Apologized in Junior High ............................. 33
God Gave Me Another Chance ............................................... 35
When Change Knocks, Allow It to Come in Your Life .......... 39
Chose to Walk on the Path of Forgiveness .............................. 44

\* \* \*

I dedicate my book to my Lord and Savior, Jesus Christ.

\* \* \*

**Never will I leave you; never will I forsake you.**

—Hebrews 13:5

# *Acknowledgments*

Without my Lord and Savior, Jesus Christ, this book wouldn't have ever been written, and for that I am grateful. Thanks for leading me and for giving my story to me to share with the world.

# *Introduction*

Bree Brown, a second-time mother, gets told by Dr. Coby Wright that her newborn, Brenaji Marshae Brown, will never walk or be able to use her hands, but God has other plans, and Brenaji ended up walking. This is proof not even doctors know everything. When Brenaji goes to school, she finds out she is different. Why has no one in her family told her she was different? Brenaji finds out about herself from a new girl that she befriended, Kimmy Timpson, and her life will be forever changed. Brenaji starts getting bullied in school in fourth grade and tells no one. It is when she gets held back in fourth grade by the principal, Mrs. Zoey Kimble, that things get worse, but little does Brenaji know there would be a new teacher, Mrs. Traneice Bowen, who is after destroying her life. Brenaji has more obstacles to face, and that is when God presents two paths to her to walk on. But what are the paths God presents to her, and which path will she walk on?

# *Welcome to My Life*

*So I wouldn't get a big head, I was given the gift of a handicap to keep me in constant touch with my limitations.*

—2 Corinthians 12:7

My name is **Brenaji Marshae Brown.** I was born on May 15, 1990, to my mother, Bree Brown, on a cold day at a hospital in California. I wasn't the only child she had. I had a two-year-old sister, Breann Brown.

I was born with deformities. I had bilateral clasped thumbs and fingers and clubbed feet. My thumbs were both bent into the palm of both my hands. Dr. Coby Wright said to my mom I would never walk due to the condition I was born with, with my feet, and he also said I wasn't going to be able to use my hands without surgery. Dr. Coby Wright referred my mom to go to the handicapped children's clinic. As a result of my deformities, I had to have surgery. Quinsy Dunn, MD, was assisted by Mike David, MD, and they both performed surgery on my clasped thumbs and deformed hands. My right hand had a more severe congenital clasped thumb. After surgery, I had to wear casts on both my hands. I had vertical talus correction done by doctors Magellan Thanh and Odom Gooding, which resulted in me wearing leg cast.

My family is from California. My granny helped my mom raise Breann and me. As I grew up, my mom was still back and forth with me in the hospital, and it wasn't easy. We relied on public transportation since my mom didn't know how to drive and didn't have a car.

There came a special point when I was back at California Hospital, and Dr. Coby Wright and I were reunited. The same doctor that said I would never walk saw me walking throughout the hospital room. He smiled from ear to ear and was in shock. He couldn't believe it—I was actually walking. My mom and my sister were the ones that saw me first walk, and Breann yelled, and I fell down, but I wasn't going to stay down forever. One day I got up and stayed on my feet and no longer fell, and I kept walking. That was proof that doctors can say one thing, and God says another thing—what a miracle. I walked and continued to walk for years without stopping. I walked with a limp, but still my limp didn't stop me from doing what was said I would never do.

In August 8, 1992, my mom had a baby boy named Byron. I wasn't treated special or as if something was wrong with me. I played with my siblings, and we all would get whipped and fussed at when we would do wrong, and we all got punished. Despite my physical disability, no family member said "Brenaji, you can't do this or that," and I'm glad they didn't. *Can't* is such a negative word. They didn't try and help me or baby me up or anything; they let me do things for myself.

But little did I know there would come a point where I no longer would just be at home with my siblings, playing and having fun. There were other places I would have to go, and school was one of them, and I would find out things about myself that not even my family told me. But why? Why had no one sat down and told me anything about myself that I didn't even know? Maybe it was better I found out on my own.

# Cali Start School

*For I know the plans I have for you, declares the Lord, plans for welfare and not for evil, to give you a future and a hope.*

—Jeremiah 29:11

In 1995, I got my first start in school at Cali Start with other kids of course. I missed home, but I had no choice but to go to this school. Even though my mom didn't have a car, I still went to school. We walked toward there, and sometimes my uncle Maine would walk with us too and carry me on his back. I learned from my mom and Uncle Maine when they would walk me to school that if you want something bad enough, don't let anything stop you to do what you have to, to achieve your goals even if you don't have a car.

I loved my teacher, Mrs. Kerry Hover. She was so sweet. I just loved being around her. She had a daughter, Macy, and she went to Cali Elementary School. Mrs. Hover took me with her to Macy's school. It was a big two-story building that was green and white. I felt like I was a big kid when I went with her to see her daughter at school, and I enjoyed myself.

I had a huge crush on a cute boy at Cali Start, Davin Porter. When you saw him, you better believe I was right beside him, smiling away like I was at the dentist's office. I loved eating breakfast and lunch around him, and he didn't even get angry that I always sat beside him—it didn't bother him one bit. His eyes were so pretty, and his smile too. We played together at recess, but never did I tell him I liked him. I told my mom and my granny that I liked Davin, and they didn't have anything to say about it. I guess to them it wasn't a big deal for a five-year-old girl liking a boy. I guess it was okay.

I loved when the photographers came to take our pictures in school, whether it was the whole class or myself. I was a true lover of the camera and was photogenic. When told "Cheese," I smiled so hard one time, making it visible to others that I had a missing tooth.

All the kids were nice except Zelda Johansen. She was so mean to me at school for no particular reason. I honestly feared her because of her unkindness toward me. My mom and I would walk to her granny's house after we got out of school, and I would be with her granny, and maybe that's where the dislike came in. Zelda's granny was crazy about me, and I was crazy about her also. At Zelda's granny's house, I swear it felt like I was home. I would get in the bed with her and hang around until it was time to go home. I honestly didn't want to go home.

Zelda just couldn't stand me—just the way that her granny talked about me made her mad with me. For no reason, Zelda started picking on me, and she hit me to the point I was in tears. I told my granny, and she talked to Zelda, and she left me alone. I honestly wished Zelda had been as nice as her granny was. Zelda was just a start when it came down to what a bully was because she wasn't the meanest, and later on, I would learn there were worse than her. She was the only kid that picked on me. Other than that, I had no problems and enjoyed my first school.

# Cali Elementary School

*I will not forget you. See I have written your name on my hand.*

—Isaiah 49:15–16

In 1996, I attended Cali Elementary School. I remembered this big green-and-white building, the same place where Mrs. Hover would bring me with her to be with Macy. I wasn't happy to be there. I wanted Mrs. Hover to be with me. I wanted to go home and just not be there.

I saw kids walking around the first day, and it made me nervous how the kids were looking at me. Maybe it was my imagination, but boy, was I afraid. I made a friend, Pracia Cunningham, who was walking with me also. My God, I got so scared I took off and ran. Kids watched as I screamed and yelled. I didn't get far though. A kindergarten teacher, Mrs. Nichelle Price, stopped me and calmed me down. Then all of a sudden, Pracia ran and screamed down the hall just like I had previously done, and this time I was watching her being calmed down just like I had been—how embarrassing. What a first day of school to remember. Maybe that was a sign that I didn't need to be at that school. I didn't belong. If I could have quit after that embarrassing day, I would've, but I was just a little kid.

I didn't have a problem making friends in school. I made friends with Don Williams. We were those friends that you would see side by side, sometimes getting in trouble for talking in class and getting fussed because we had a lot to talk about when Ms. Gloria Conerly was talking.

Our teacher, Ms. Conerly, was an older lady. When she would walk, you could hear her bones pop all of a sudden. She was not nice. I stayed in time-out the most in kindergarten. I got in trouble with Marie Trosclair. She walked up to me and cut a hole in my shirt for no reason, and I cut a hole back in her shirt. Ms. Conerly taped both our shirts back together. I was so upset that I burst out in tears, and Ms. Conerly told me to get in time-out. I sat in time-out with my hands covering my face. At recess, Ms. Conerly took my candy away because Breann saw me eating candy, she wanted to know who gave me snack money, and I refused to tell her. Then she asked me for some candy, and I told her no. I wasn't sharing with her, and she was not happy that I was being greedy. Ms. Conerly took my candy away from me after the big commotion with my sister and me. She didn't return it. I felt she must have eaten it herself—how mean and greedy.

There were several fun times I had in kindergarten. For Halloween, I remember we were allowed to wear costumes, and I was a cute Indian. My mom sent me to class with a bag of candy, and Ms. Conerly passed out everybody's candy. We had a lot of stuff and snacks. For Thanksgiving, there were teepees outside, and the kindergarteners got to feast, and we got all types of stuff. At Christmas time, Ms. Conerly told the class the story about the gingerbread man. She said he had ran all over the school, and we went walking down the hallway in search of the gingerbread man. I didn't see the gingerbread man running at all. I figured he was just that quick I couldn't capture him. After we returned from looking for the gingerbread man, he was on the table. Ms. Conerly sliced it, and it was so yummy. For Mardi Gras, the school had a parade outside but a mini version for us kids. We got to eat my favorite king cake, and when you got the baby in your slice of king cake, you had to bring the next king cake. When Easter came, I couldn't go to school because I had chicken pox, so Breann went to Ms. Conerly's classroom and got my Easter basket and brought it home to me. The class went on a field trip to the zoo. It was so nice just looking at animals. I loved nap time—all the kindergarteners were on mats on the floor—but one day, Ms. Conerly's caterpillar got out. It was in my spot—thank God it didn't sting me. She turned on the lights just in time.

In the morning, we would sing songs in class and dance too; one song that I loved dearly was "Twinkle, Twinkle, Little Star." We read stories in class, and I liked this one story "The Stinky Cheese Man." No one wanted to be bothered by this nonfictional story character. They wouldn't run behind him, but from him, because he had a horrible odor.

I got held back by Ms. Conerly, so I had to spend another year with her. The time went by fast. It wasn't bad at all. I finally made it to first grade after two years of kindergarten, which felt like forever.

In first grade, I saw something I never saw before while standing in line in the hallway talking to some classmates. A teacher, Mrs. Kami Vicknair, looked like her body was hurting her, and she walked with a noticeable limp. My classmates and I were having a conversation about the songs that we would sing, and we were laughing so hard that Marcia Kemp told our teacher, Mrs. Eli Newman, that we were all making fun of Mrs. Vicknair when nobody was. I didn't even get an opportunity to tell Mrs. Newman what we were laughing at, and she lowered our conduct just because of Marcia's lie. I wasn't raised to make fun of anybody. It hurt more than anything because Marcia wanted me to get in trouble, and just what she wanted, she got. That was the first time I ever got in trouble in Mrs. Newman's class.

I was normally quiet in class. I did participate in class and did all my homework. I loved school, and I kept up my grades. Second and third grade were very exciting moments in my life. I was an A–B honor roll student. I was Student of the Month both years and went to parties for those that made the honor roll. I was encouraged to keep up the good work. I would get money from family members, and that also made me work harder. Besides, I loved using the money I got to buy snacks in school.

In third grade, the class went to the YMCA for a field trip, and we were getting taught how to swim. I was trying to catch on but struggled. Markeith Thump swam where I was. He challenged me to go underneath the water with him to see who would come up faster, and I took the challenge. He beat me to it; we started laughing about the situation, since I came up last. The next day at school, Markeith had his friend Todd Wilks tell me that he liked me. I politely told Todd I didn't like Markeith. I didn't lie. I just told Todd the truth. But Markeith had something up his sleeve, and it was just for me. I accepted the fact that not everybody that you like may not like you back, but not everybody was like me or felt the way I did.

I just had one more year left to go—fourth grade was the last grade and then off to middle school, at least I thought. I may have felt sad in Cali Start about Zelda picking on me and thought the first day of kindergarten was horrible, but little did I know fourth grade was going to change my life forever.

# Fourth Grade

*Jesus said, "In this world you will have trouble. But take heart! I have overcome the world."*

—John 16:33

In 1999, I was in fourth grade, and things were great. Friends weren't a problem; I had a friend, Raymira Stokes. We were close and hung together, not just at school but also outside of school. I was excited to be in class with my crush, Davin. I still remained quiet about my feelings for him. We got a new student at the beginning of the school year, Nya Smolder. She and I became friends. Nya didn't wear uniforms like everyone else—I don't know why—but she didn't. She wore shorts a lot, and they were too short. Boys looked at her, and they liked her. I was hurt one day when I saw Davin and her flirting on the bench at recess. I was walking toward them, and I turned around and went another direction. I was sad, and it broke my heart. No one knew. I kept it buried inside. I didn't even tell Nya that I liked Davin. Nya and Davin ended up dating each other. I had no choice but to get over him. I remained friends with Nya anyway, and it wasn't like Davin and I were a couple.

There were some mean girls, Anaya Stone and May Letterman, in class. I was quiet and stayed on my best behavior, but all of a sudden, they started to pick on me. Ms. Ria Anthony had us in groups. We were painting for fun, and both of them were in the group with me. I accidentally splashed paint on my shirt as well as Anaya's shirt, and May said aloud, "Brenaji would be washing my shirt and drying it too, but I doubt she can even afford a washer or a dryer to dry it."

I slumped down in my seat. I wanted to cry so bad because I didn't do it on purpose. I made a mistake. I couldn't even say sorry, but I was very sorry. I wouldn't have done that intentionally to anyone.

Anaya would just pick on me for just about anything. She would call me "Baldhead Scallywag Ain't Got No Hair in the Back." It came from this song by Project Pat called "Chicken Head." Several days, Anaya would just say "Uggghh" to me, and so did May, and I wouldn't respond to it. It hurt.

There were days I sat in class and cried. I just put my head down so nobody would see my face because my classmates would pick on me. One day, my mom showed up to school to my dismay, and I was crying, but I had my head down so no one would see my face. Bobby Gomez was the one that told me my mom was at school. If he hadn't said a word, my mom might have seen what was going on. I hurried and wiped the tears away before my mom came in the classroom. I put on a happy face, but little did she know I wasn't happy. I was hiding and was hurt.

Every day I faced something new, and sometimes I just wanted to run away and disappear off the face of the earth. All the mistreatment hurt so bad.

Ms. Anthony introduced us to this new girl named Kimmy Timpson, and little did I know she would change my life forever. Kimmy and I became close friends instantly. We were inseparable— when you saw her, you saw me. It wasn't long that rumors in school started to spread that Kimmy and I were gay. In the cafeteria, at lunchtime, I overheard Kizzi Parks and Marcia Kemp both saying that Kimmy and I were gay. Even Toby Miller said the same thing aloud. I had no response to the gay rumors. They did not know I was sitting at the table behind them, nor did they care if I heard them. I kept it to myself and told no one. Not even the teacher, the principal, my mom, Granny—just no one. Marcia, Kizzi, and I used to hang together. We were all honor roll students, and I felt they were upset that I hung around them less and Kimmy more. I felt like they thought they were better than the other children who didn't make honor roll like we all would. They acted sidity.

The class left for recess when Kimmy got upset; I don't remember why she was upset. That's all I remember. She pointed to my hands and said to me, "Brenaji with your cripple-hand self."

I heard those hurtful words that caused me to look at myself differently. It felt like she had stabbed me with a knife in my heart, and it hurt that bad. I knew then I was different, but never was I told this. My eyes were filled with tears, but I couldn't even cry. I lost a lot of things that day: my friend, my self-esteem, and so much more.

Things for me only got worse. A lot of my classmates were no longer my friends; they excluded me, and I felt so alone. They didn't play with me at recess anymore. I no longer made the A–B honor roll. It was only Raymira that remained my friend. She has never treated me bad, ever.

My mornings changed. I went from liking to go to school to actually hating going altogether. My mom would wake me up because she had to catch the transit bus before I went to school. When she would wake me, I would hurry and get back in bed but had no choice but to go. I didn't tell my mom why I didn't want to go to school or that I didn't.

Lamont Gateaux dropped his pencil, and I leaned down to pick it up, and he yelled out "Don't touch my pencil!" I swear it was because of the way my hands were. I wished I could have changed myself so children would have accepted me. Maybe the ones that picked on me would've been nicer to me.

Still things got worse. I was so stressed out and tired of everything. We had to take the LEAP Test to go onto fifth grade. I took it and failed it by three points. The principal (Mrs. Zoey Kimble) was the one who could decide to let me go on to fifth grade. She chose not to let me go on, but I could go to summer school and retake the LEAP Test. I went to summer school, and it wasn't fun. The teacher, Mrs. Trinity Clark—I swear she had serious issues. She would fuss at me because I had a habit of messing with my fingernails when she was at the board going over math, and it wasn't on purpose. When it was time to go home, I was made fun of by Jetta Cordeaux because of the way I ran when I got off the bus. I had no control of the way I ran or even walked.

Omari King and Don Jay Marts caught me off guard another day while riding the bus. With the fact that the road was bumpy and I couldn't hear what Omari was asking me, I simply replied no. What had I said no to? Both Omari and Don Jay burst out into laughter. He asked me did I take baths.

I was not surprised because children would say just anything to me, and never did I bother them. My life was a joke to so many— either they were making fun of my disability or saying cruel stuff just for the fun of it.

I still didn't make it when I retested. I was kept in fourth grade by just three points. Mrs. Kimble could have let me go on but still chose not to.

# The Repeat of Fourth Grade

*Fear not, for I am with you; do not be dismayed, for I am your God. I will strengthen you and help you; I will uphold you with my righteous right hand.*
—Isaiah 41:10

In 2000, I was in fourth grade again. My good friend Raymira had passed and went on to fifth grade. She didn't know I didn't make it until the first day of school. Breann came home and told me Raymira asked where I was, and she told her I did not pass. I wanted this all to be a dream, but it wasn't. It was real, and I had to be in fourth grade this time again, but it would be like a nightmare.

There was a new teacher, Mrs. Traneice Bowen, in the place of Ms. Ria Anthony since she retired from school. Mrs. Bowen was a darkskinned lady who wore red lipstick. Her ears were holy, her fingers had rings on all of them, and she had her hair short at the top and long in the back, and you could see through it since it was so thin. She also had a visible mustache you couldn't help but notice. Mrs. Bowen taught math and spelling.

Things were okay at first until the incident in the library. Mrs. Matric Morris, the librarian, and my classmates left, leaving Jorden Booker and me alone in the library. When we were left alone, he asked me to let him feel underneath my dress, and I told him no. He got so mad that he turned red in his face. I didn't tell anyone, and I knew it wasn't right what he asked me. Jorden wasn't through with me after I declined what he had asked. He was after making my life hell, and that was just what he would do.

All of a sudden, Jorden started picking on me in class. And not only was it him, but it was a gang of them after a while—Bryson Sherith, Ted Martin, Brendon Valmont, Tyrone Kidd, Garla Stein, and Ruston Tillman. Jorden mocked me on how I walked. The shoes I wore, he referred to them as roach steppers. He told me my hands were so crippled I could direct a band with them, and he told me I was ugly. The other boys called me names too. I was called handicap, ugly, cripple, cripple fingers. They told me I was doing the crip walk when I walked, and this was an everyday thing unless I was absent from school.

Mrs. Bowen heard them loud and clear. They would throw erasers and paper balls at me in class, and nobody got in trouble for doing that either. Mrs. Bowen would not stop them from doing anything. It was me who got fussed at for telling them to stop. Don, the girl that I had been friends with from kindergarten, even picked on me. She would call me butterball aloud in class, and God knows I wasn't even fat. Mrs. Bowen saw Brendon just walk up to me and push me down on the floor, and even though she saw it, she didn't tell him a thing.

I told my granny about Brendon pushing me, and she called Brendon's granny's house to speak with his mom, Aretha. She wasn't there, and she never returned the phone calls or the messages that Brendon's sister, Lauren, got from my granny to give to her. My granny just wanted him to leave me alone. She wanted to do things the right way.

Brendon told me, "Your granny calls, and you think my mom does me something. Well, she doesn't do me a thing," and he smiled.

I believed every word he said too.

In class, Garla Stein just looked at me and said, "Brenaji, I know what your hands look like. I could imagine what your feet look like."

When I tried to stand up for myself, Mrs. Bowen would get mad. She took my bullies' side, and I had no voice. There were days when the class had a test to take, and my bullies would pick on me worse. I would stand up to them and beg them to leave me alone, but they wouldn't—they would continue.

Mrs. Bowen did the unthinkable. She told me to get out of the classroom and on a test day—not the children that bullied me, but me. I did as I was told. I didn't sass her; I got out. Before I got out of the classroom, she put my test down on the desk I had sat in and wrote with a red pen on it a large red *F*. *F* stands for failure, and I felt just like I was a failure. I couldn't learn, and I lost interest. It was all because of the bullying. I swear it felt like somebody had stomped all over my brain. I wasn't allowed to take my test at all because I stood up for myself.

I remember when I was actually in class when Brendon told Mrs. Bowen she had a mustache, and never had I ever told her such a thing. I just knew he would get punished, but she simply said "I know" with a smile on her face and laughed. If that were me, I would've been put out of school—or worse yet, sent to jail. Brendon got the right of way with her, which was so unfair.

Mrs. Bowen put me out of class almost every day after that test day. I stood in the hallway days before she ever thought about putting a desk in the hallway for me to sit in. She knew I had a physical handicap. It hurt just to stand up too long. I cried. It hurt so bad, and all I wanted was help. I wanted the bullying to stop. After a while, Mrs. Bowen just would kick me out of class as soon as I walked in the door. Mrs. Bowen decided to put a desk in the hallway for me to sit in. It was actually roomy and comfy. A few days later, she walked out in the hall with a desk too small and exchanged it with the one that I was sitting in, and boy, did I cry like a baby, and the children humiliated me.

The teasing only got worse. I didn't know if I was going to make it. My classmates came out of class, and so many of them—especially Bryson, Brendon, and Jorden—loved seeing me suffer. They would tell me not to touch them because they didn't want to catch what I had, and in my face, they would burst out in laughter at the sight of me outside class in a small desk and crying because I wanted to be left alone.

I went home hiding everything; I could not tell it. I cried myself to sleep every night, but I made sure everybody was asleep, and I would be praying and asking God to take me away. I didn't want to live. Maybe God would answer my prayers, and I would be free. I felt there was no point in me living—nobody liked me. I didn't know anything about suicide, but if I did, I would've killed myself. I had no reason to live. I was hated.

Mrs. Bowen was my bully, and just like my classmates, she added to the suffering I had already faced. She started writing me up, and I ended up in the principal's office. Some afternoons when it was almost time to go home, Mrs. Bowen's twelfth-grade daughter, Tracey, would come to her class until it was time to go home. Tracey was something else too. She acted very nasty toward me, and she had no right to. I was a child, but not hers. It's true what they say, "The apple doesn't fall that far from the tree."

Mrs. Zoey Kimble, the principal, was a brown-skinned, heavyset woman who wore small glasses below her nose. She also wore red lipstick, and her hair was a dark-blonde color. I told her about the bullying and all that was going on, but she did nothing. She made things worse—she started paddling me just because I stood up to my bullies. I was being punished, and I was the victim. No one tried to help me or cared about me.

On the way home from school, Lisette Penelope decided to pick on Byron. I told her to leave my brother alone, and she said, "Yeah, that's why your mama ain't got no teeth."

I said, "Well, at least my mama got pretty legs," and I stood up on the bus and pulled my pant legs up and showed her my legs.

The children on the bus made an uproar after I stood up to her. I was only doing what was right.

The next day in the morning, my name was called to the office, then Lisette and the bus driver Mrs. Ricco Phillis hadn't driven on the grounds of the school well enough when we were both called. Lisette's mom called Mrs. Kimble on the phone and told on me, but I only wanted her to leave my brother alone. We both went into the office, and Mrs. Kimble, to no surprise, sided with Lisette.

I still was having a hard time, and still I went to Mrs. Kimble about the bullying. She said to me, "Brenaji, your handicap is like my weight, it can't be changed." That was a lie, and I wasn't stupid. She could lose weight, and if I would lose weight, still I would have a handicap.

Later on that day, I was sitting in class and Mrs. Bowen walked up to me and saw I had a picture on my desk. It was of my little brother. She picked it up and walked away with it toward the garbage can, and she tore it up piece by piece. The tears just rolled down my cheeks. I couldn't say a thing. She didn't know if my brother was dead or alive to do such a thing—or worse yet, she couldn't care less. She was after hurting me as if I wasn't already suffering.

At recess, I started hanging by myself. I stood up against a fence and held onto it, and I would look at my bullies playing and nobody wanted to be my friend. Nobody liked me. It was enough knowing that the girls that I thought were my friends—Don was talking on the phone with Kimmy—talked about my hair, saying I didn't have any hair. They didn't know I heard them. I hung up and cried.

I was written up by Mrs. Bowen so much that I stayed downstairs on the outside of Mrs. Kimble's office on a yellow bench and cried. Sitting outside the office, I even overheard Mrs. Kimble, and she was talking about me to a special aid teacher, Mrs. Kori Falls, telling her I was a troubled child. Mrs. Falls wasn't even my teacher. Mrs. Falls told Mrs. Kimble that Mrs. Ronda Vandyke would beat me because of my behavior, but there was no teacher there by that name. Maybe Mrs. Vandyke was Mrs. Falls's principal, but it sounded horrible, more like abuse. The only thing I was doing was seeking help, but with the way things were, I was the problem.

If I wasn't on the yellow bench or in that small desk, I would be sitting in detention with this older lady, Mrs. Norcia Hooks, and she had an evil look in her. The class was dark, it somewhat gave me the creeps and smelled funny. I sat in detention and would write one hundred times, "I will not disrupt the class." That was my punishment. My hands would hurt so bad, more so because of my disability.

I did what I had to do. I was punished just for asking for bullies to leave me alone. Mrs. Kimble even had the cop, Mr. Randy Surge, come for me. She wanted me to go to jail, but the jailhouse was full. She said she wished they had a cell so I could go.

Mrs. Kimble finally decided that I should get some help, and she sent me to see a counselor at the school, Mrs. Sandy Conair. She was once a teacher, and I had heard some bad stuff about her, that she threw books at students in her class, and that scared me. I thought a counselor's job is to give guidance on personal or psychological problems. Mrs. Conair was a noisy woman, and she was no help.

I got off the school bus, and I saw my granny hanging clothes on the line, and I told her about the bullying. Things hadn't changed.

Every day it got worse. For once, I felt things would get better after I told my granny. I sat at the table at home and asked my granny, "Am I handicapped?" and she said yes. Why hadn't anyone told me this? Maybe if I had been told it, it wouldn't hurt to be called handicapped. My granny came to the school to talk about the bullying with Mrs. Kimble, but Mrs. Kimble had an attitude as if she couldn't care less. As my granny was getting ready to leave, she said Mrs. Conair said that I had asked about sex. It was a lie. I hadn't asked about sex. I couldn't care less about any talks of sex.

I worried if I was going to ever get a break from bullying. Would I live or die—that was my concern.

My granny told Mrs. Kimble that she no longer wanted me to be counseled by Mrs. Conair, she didn't want me counseled there anymore.

It was enough that I refused to eat in the cafeteria because I didn't want to be around my bullies. They would bully me sitting on the bench by Mrs. Kimble's office anyway. I didn't have to say anything to anybody even sitting on the bench. Joni Price and Huey Marston both were passing by and looked down at my hands and said, "Your hands look funny and so creepy." I hated my hands. I tried to hide them, but it was too late. They all saw my hands.

It caught me by surprise one morning that Mrs. Bowen let me go in class with my classmates. The class had a spelling test, and she graded our test. Everybody did well on it. Afterward, Mrs. Bowen went to her desk and got a jar filled with bubblegum all the way to the top. She passed the gum out to everybody, even me. She allowed us to eat our gum in class. I unwrapped my gum and put it in my mouth and started chewing, but before I knew it, Mrs. Bowen walked up to me and said loudly, "You don't deserve any gum. Spit it out." I did as I was told even though I hadn't done anything wrong. I wanted to cry, but I held back my tears. The only thing that made me happy was when the bell rang to go home.

My granny and my sister were in the living room when I ran through the house after getting off the school bus. I cried out, "I can't take it anymore!"

I overheard Breann say to my granny, "What's wrong with Naji?"

My granny walked up to me and asked what was wrong. I threw my backpack on the kitchen floor and cried loudly, and I told her how bad things had gotten and how Mrs. Bowen would pick on me.

My granny spoke with Mrs. Kimble again, but this time about how Mrs. Bowen was treating me so badly. After my granny talked to Mrs. Kimble, the whole fourth-grade class was questioned. Was Mrs. Bowen treating me bad, and did they see her treating me bad? All my classmates said the same thing one by one in front of Mrs. Kimble and the ones I thought were my friends also: "No."

I couldn't believe it. I felt like I was in hell. Nobody but God knew the truth, but my granny believed me.

After that, nothing changed. I still would get treated bad as well as bullied.

I took the LEAP Test and passed it. God knows I don't know how, with all the hell I was going through, but it was God. Nothing got resolved at that school.

The summertime came, and I cried every night because I was so afraid to go to Cali Middle School. I was scared the bullying would be worse, and I was worried about the type of principal I would have. Maybe the bullies would be too big for me and would physically hurt me this time. I just didn't know what to think. I didn't want to ever go back to school again. God knows I wondered, Why me? What did I do to be treated so badly? When would the pain stop?

# *Heading to Cali Middle School*

*This trouble you're in isn't punishment; its training, the normal experience of children ... God is doing what is best for us, training us to live God's holy best.*

—Hebrews 12:8, 10

In 2002, I made it to middle school as a fifth grader. There was a new principal the year I arrived there. The new principal, Mrs. Sasha Darinsky, was a light-skinned lady with curly short hair. She was skinny, and she too wore red lipstick just like Mrs. Kimble and Mrs. Bowen. My God, I felt like it meant something by them wearing red lipstick—evilness, just evil. I judged Mrs. Darinsky before I got to know her.

It came to me that this time around, I had to fight for my rights even if it meant for me to get into trouble. No way was I going to be picked on, even if it were by Mrs. Darinsky herself. I was not going to back down to her. That she didn't have a paddle to hit me like Mrs. Kimble did was the only difference so far.

I didn't even try to hang with Raymira when I made it to Cali Middle. I missed our friendship, but the damage was done; life itself had gone on. She made more friends. I couldn't even talk to her, let alone say anything. I was not the same after repeating fourth grade. My life changed drastically. Anything was expected from me.

One morning while waiting outside with Roque Walker (my new neighbor), a black car slowed down, and I thought nothing of it because cars pass by all the time. The car got closer, and Mrs. Kimble opened the door on the passenger side and looked at me and asked if I liked my new school. I politely said yes, and she had the nerve to smile as if she didn't treat me bad, but what was she up to?

It wasn't long before I started to get into trouble at Cali Middle. Mrs. Cerald Seinfeld was the only one out of my fifth-grade teachers that I actually opened up to and told about how mean children treated me, and she allowed me to sit in class but on the opposite side of my classmates. She even told me she was on my side, but I felt lonely and left out and eventually joined my classmates.

Not long after I moved to the other side of the class, the bullying began. Ted Martin started talking trash about my mama at recess, and I took my foot and kicked him in his knee. He called Mrs. Darinsky and told her what I had done. She fussed at me and told me, "I don't like your attitude." I said back to her, "I don't like yours either," then Mrs. Darinsky said, "Get in the office." I did as I was told. I walked to the office and waited for her to come, and when she did, she assigned me to go to detention.

Who was I, and what happened to the quiet girl that I once was? Who was this angry, heartless person I had become? I wasn't one to fight back and was not a troublemaker. I wanted the old me back, but the damage was done. This mean girl was me now. I made a huge change. I was a badass—at least I thought so.

I was so bold that I even skipped detention when I knew I had to go, but I didn't get away with it. Mrs. Darinsky called my name over the intercom, "Brenaji Brown, report to the office," not once but twice. When I made it to the office, she asked why I hadn't gone to detention. I lied to her and said, "I forgot." I knew what I was doing.

She told me, "Brenaji, you better not forget again."

I never did that again. I went to detention like I was supposed to.

I saw a seventh grader, Walton Davies. He was tall and dark skinned with pretty teeth. He wore his hair braided to the back. I had a crush on him. He didn't know. I don't know who found out, but they told him, and he said he didn't like me, which hurt my feelings. Walton had a bad side to him, and his name was called to the office almost every day because he stayed in trouble. After a while, he just was no longer at Cali Middle.

My grades were As and Bs and one C—always in math. I always missed the honor roll, but did I care? Nope, not anymore. The subject I focused on was bullying. I was written up a lot for standing up to my bullies.

Markeith and Todd, were now sixth graders, got in my face at recess, and God knows they couldn't sing one good tune. If they were ever on the Apollo Show, they would've been booed off immediately because they had not been born with the gift to be singers. They sounded worse than two cats fighting. They burst out into a song and sung "All My Life I Been Po'" by Nappy Roots. I'm sure this song wasn't made to make fun of people like it was used against me. I wasn't rich. Even if I were, I wouldn't have made fun of other people to hurt them. Markeith was just mad that I rejected him in elementary school, and that was his way of getting back at me by hurting me. Markeith didn't know that only made me dislike him.

Townshend Jones saw what was going on with me with the bullies at school and on the bus. He was also a sixth grader, but he was not a fan of the whole bullying thing. He told my bullies to leave me alone. Townshend told me, "Brenaji, if you need me to come in the office, I will be too glad to come and be your witness." What a kind thing to do to show that you care. I felt good knowing there were a few people that actually didn't like seeing me suffer.

I got into so much trouble that I missed out on lots of activities in school, all because I didn't want to be around my classmates. The class went on all types of trips, and I stayed back at school while they all were having fun. It didn't bother me that they were gone. I couldn't even ride my original school bus anymore because I would get teased so badly.

My granny asked our neighbor Mr. John Cole if I could ride his bus, and she told him how I was being bullied. He was too glad to help out. I rode the bus with Mr. Cole when he would pick up the elementary kids. I sat far behind on that bus, and I observed the little kids on the bus. I still was riding the bus with children I went to school with, but nobody teased me. I felt so much better.

In Mrs. Seinfeld's fifth-grade class, Ruston Tillman came in after recess, and he imitated the way I walked and said that was the way I walked—he said, "The Crip Walk"—and he burst out into laughter. Even some of my classmates laughed with him too. I got so upset and told him, "Go to hell, Ruston," and the class said, "Awwwww." Mrs. Seinfeld wasn't in the class, yet they said they were going to tell, and they did just that. Mrs. Seinfeld wrote me up. The only thing was Mrs. Darinsky was absent that day.

The secretary, Mrs. Faith Cole, let me know I was going to end up going to Anger Ville. Anger Ville was a place you would go if you were getting into trouble and had lots of write-ups in school. I was scared. I had never been there before.

I went home to my granny and told her what all that happened at school. The bullying was so bad that I felt it was eating me alive, but when it got out of hand, I had no choice but to get help. I was afraid. My granny caught a ride to the school the next day.

Everything was so familiar. I went with my granny before when she went that time with Mrs. Kimble, and nothing happened—things got worse. But this was not Mrs. Kimble—this was Mrs. Darinsky. My granny told her what was going on with the bullying and told her I was physically handicapped.

Mrs. Darinsky said she wasn't going to have this going on. She said to me, "Brenaji, let me know when you get bullied, and I will deal with the bullies—the same goes for you."

Wait—Mrs. Darinsky was not after hurting me, but actually, she was going to help me. Mrs. Darinsky changed her mind. I wasn't going to Anger Ville after all. She told my granny that she had heard about me, which was no surprise; I'm sure it was that Mrs. Kimble. She kept my name in her mouth like a piece of food. My God, I felt so relieved. I still didn't trust Mrs. Darinsky though.

The bullying still went on. I stopped going outside for recess, and I ended up going to the library instead and read *Chicken Soup for the Teenage Soul* books. They comforted me and gave me hope that I would survive bullying. It started off as one day of going to the library to escape bullying to days.

I even reached out online. I was searching and saw something about writing for children, and there were questions I filled out and a spot to submit a short story. I submitted my story about my life with bullying. I got a phone call from a lady named Brenda Clay, and she had my story. She asked me if what I wrote was true, and I told her yes.

She went on to tell me her daughter was going through something, and she felt my story could help her daughter, so she took my story home to her daughter.

From that day on, I wanted to help others. I didn't have the money to write a book, so I just let my dream go. Even though I couldn't afford to pay to publish a book, still I never forgot about it. I would find myself writing poems and actually loving writing altogether.

When Mrs. Shalita Parfait, the librarian, wasn't at school, the library would be closed, and that saddened me, leaving me no choice but to be outside with the children that bullied me. I had some friends that I played with: Tiffany Wilks and Tyriqua Saint. They were nice to me.

You would think when the school year came to an end, I would be free of bullying, but that wasn't the case. My mom enrolled my siblings and me in summer camp over the summer. My next-door neighbor, Mrs. Lauretha Chestnut, was so kind to bring us to camp since her daughter Juliet was going to. I hated camp—just to be around the children that bullied me in school was enough. When I saw Jorden at camp, that was it for me. I could've gone back home.

I saw Walton at camp, and I didn't say anything to him. I overheard Walton telling Joni I was ugly. He said it so loud that others could hear him.

I was getting ready to answer Walton when Drake Matthews, an older boy, said, "You're not all that good-looking yourself, Walton, and you need to look in the mirror."

I was shocked, more than anything, that anyone would take up with me. Joni was mad that Drake took up with me. Drake and Joni were actually cousins.

Drake told him, "I'm going to tell Auntie Liza on you. You know she doesn't play with you."

Nothing was said after Drake spoke. I couldn't even say thank you because, more than anything, I was still in shock. I felt good afterward. I admired Drake because he didn't just sit around and say nothing when I was being picked on. He made me feel better.

# Sixth Grade

*The Lord will work out his plans for my life.*

—Psalm 138:8

In 2003, I was a sixth grader. At recess, I was walking past a fifth grader, Carlton Rivers, and he said, "Oooohh" when he saw me. It didn't bother me one bit, I didn't even question him. I guess Carlton was shy because he had his good friend Mennis Walcott to tell me the next day at recess that he liked me. I didn't even say I liked Carlton; I didn't say anything.

Carlton started attending the church I attended, California Baptist Church, and he saw me at choir rehearsal. I was in the youth choir. Carlton flirted with me in school and talked about how I looked clapping in choir. He even imitated my clapping and smiled at me. He would come to the church I attended more after seeing me there. I started to like Carlton, but I was so shy.

I went to physical therapy a lot, and I would be gone more than being at school. My therapist was Candice Tipton, and she worked on my foot and hands. I ended up getting hand braces made for my hands, and I had my shoes fixed so that I wouldn't limp when I walked. It was enough children made fun of the way that I walked; I ended up hurting myself just to please them by not wearing my shoes.

Maybe I wore my shoes five times and put them away. I found myself telling Candice about life for me in school, how children would make fun of me and call me names.

She told me to tell them, "I am rubber, and you are glue. Whatever you say bounces off me and sticks to you."

I stood up for myself. I wasn't going to let anyone make me feel like I was nobody ever again. The sixth-grade teachers would have to get used to it.

I got so tired of the bullying that one day I got back at one bully, Tyrone Kidd. He always was telling me I was ugly and laughing in my face. He reminded me that I was crippled—either that or he was hitting me. The class was going to the computer lab, and I stepped on Tyrone's shoe purposely. I was fighting back for all those times he picked on me. Tyrone told me to stop, but I didn't. I kept it up. I kept it up so much that he turned around and slapped me in my face, and you heard the lick echo in the hallway. I didn't respond. Boy, did that lick hurt.

We made it in the computer lab. I slapped Tyrone back, and he slapped me again. Then we stood before our classmates like we were in a ring. We were repeatedly slapping each other. The substitute, Mrs. Derince Whitaker, looked so scared she pulled the string to the office. Tyrone and I were both walked down to the office. We both had to attend Saturday school as our punishment. Mr. Ron Bowen was the teacher whose class we were in for punishment. He knew I had a physical handicap somehow, and he refused to let me do the exercises because of it. That was my first and last time going to Saturday school.

I felt the need to make a change. I was no longer sassy with Mrs. Darinsky, because she was on my side and looked out for me. More than anything, she was a fair principal. I misjudged her all because of what I went through with my elementary principal, Mrs. Kimble. I thought she too would be the same, but I was so wrong. I actually liked Mrs. Darinsky and what she stood for. Mrs. Darinsky would walk in the class at any time, and that was a good thing. If anyone was doing something wrong, she would see it—even me. She was a concerned principal.

I started enjoying school again and did better altogether. Mrs. Gloria Greendale started sending my mom notes about my behavior, and I would read them, and she had a lot of good things to say about me and my behavior. There was a program called the Seven Habits that some students were pulled out of class to be a part of, and I was one of the students. The seven habits program was good for me. I gained self-confidence, I began to believe in myself, and I no longer believed the stuff I was told by children to hurt me.

Just because I was in the program to help me, that didn't mean the bullies would stop bullying me. It took a new girl, Harriet James, who stayed in all sorts of trouble to pick on me worse. We never said a word to each other. One day, however, we eyeballed each other in the hallway, but we didn't say anything. I was outside at recess passing by the basketball court and accidently got in the way of Harriet.

She screamed out to me, "You handicapped bitch!" and Huey, who was standing beside her, burst out in laughter.

I didn't argue with Harriet. I learned in the seven habits program to be proactive instead of reactive. It hurt, but I did what I had to do. I went to the office, but Mrs. Darinsky was not at school to be told about what happened with Harriet. Mrs. Darinsky was at school the next day, and she had gotten my message about what happened with Harriet. Let's just say Harriet got into trouble, then she ended up moving away.

I wasn't arguing with anyone in class and getting into any more trouble. It was peaceful for me. I was doing what Mrs. Darinsky had told me, telling on the children that picked on me. I also started seeing the counselor, Mrs. Alissa Thibodaux. She was a sweet lady. I remember asking her about magazines she had in her office by Joyce Meyer that I would read when I would go to her. Mrs. Thibodaux told me how to go by getting those magazines so I could have them sent to me at home since they were of help to me.

I wanted help, and I was getting what I needed. I saw change in myself and change in my behavior most importantly. I started to participate in stuff in school. The bazaar for Halloween was my favorite. I had so much fun. I felt like the nicer me had come back; I felt so freed.

My teacher, Mrs. Ella Little, was the one who said, "Brenaji, I'm not supposed to be telling you this, but you're getting an award." In my mind I was like, *OMG, I'm getting an award*. She told me because I almost got into trouble, but thank God I didn't.

The day of the award ceremony, I wanted to cry tears of joy, but I didn't. I thought about all that I had been through and how I went in with an attitude, but I developed a positive one. I misjudged Mrs. Darinsky but made a change because of her. Those happy days would come to an end very soon and unexpectedly. It's unfair, but everything in life that God does is for a reason. It's when things are going good that something always happens so suddenly.

Over the summer, I experienced my first kiss with Carlton. He happened to be next door at his cousin's house fishing when he saw me and came my way. He was wearing blue shorts and a white T-shirt and was wearing brown sandals. I had on a purple shirt with a purple flower hairband in my head to match, and

I wore blue capris with my purple flower sandals when Carlton asked me for a kiss. I was nervous more than anything because I had never kissed a boy. We went to stand at the side of the house. He stood in front of me and looked at me, and we smiled at each other. I remember just closing my eyes and feeling his soft lips on mine. Our kiss lasted a few seconds, and it wasn't bad for my first time.

Breann and our neighbor Kira Philips were there, and they knew about our kiss and watched out for me that I wouldn't get caught kissing.

I didn't tell anyone. I didn't tell my granny about it either. It was just a special moment for me.

# She Left Me

*Jesus weeps at the sight of you. Not tears of shame but tears of joy. He calls for you. "Come to me, all of you who are weary and carry heavy burdens, and I will give you rest."*

—Matthew 11:28

In 2004 when I went back to school, Mrs. Darinsky was no longer principal. God knew what he was doing when he sent Mrs. Darinsky to Cali Middle School. I felt that he sent her as help for me. I got peace in the short time she was there. I wish I had known Mrs. Darinsky was no longer going to be there for my seventh-grade year, and it felt like somebody died. I missed her. I cried that day when I got home. I felt like things would get bad again. I just wanted Mrs. Darinsky back. She went on to be principal at another school, but I wanted her to stay. She was there for me, and I got my break with her there as principal. I wished it had all been a dream, but it wasn't—she wasn't coming back as principal.

There was another principal, Mrs. Angela Belle. She was a brown-skinned woman. She didn't wear makeup, and she was not fat or skinny but in between.

I found out something interesting about one of my seventh-grade teachers, Mr. Bowen, who taught social studies. It didn't ring a bell nor had I ever thought about it, but Mr. Bowen said his wife was a teacher too. Mrs. Bowen, my fourth-grade teacher, was his wife. His daughter looked like a combination of both her parents but more like Mrs. Bowen with Mr. Bowen's complexion. I found out by overhearing my classmates Crashante Barrow and Viviane Stewart, who also were in Mrs. Bowen's fourth-grade class with me. I guess it's true what they say, opposites do attract. I didn't ever say or ask Mr. Bowen about Mrs. Bowen—I wasn't interested—nor did I tell him she was my fourth grade teacher.

Mr. Bowen was actually a nice teacher, but whatever you do, don't say *corn* or you'll get into trouble. Mr. Bowen told the class the story why he hated the word *corn*. As a punishment when he was younger, they had to get on their knees in corn and face toward the wall, and it hurt. I had no reason to talk about corn and avoided any talks of corn so I wouldn't get into trouble.

Mr. Bowen never treated me bad like his wife had. That's probably how he knew I had a disability, from Mrs. Bowen. He would let the class go outside if we completed our assignments early. Mr. Bowen excused me from the activities without a doctor's excuse. I can definitely say Mr. Bowen did have a mean look to him, but looks are so deceiving.

His class was the class I looked forward to going to. It was fun. I enjoyed the assignments we had. One of my favorite assignments that he had the class do was for black history month. He picked someone for everyone in the class. I got the gospel singer, Mahalia Jackson, and I had never heard of her. I no longer had a computer at home because our dog, Prince, bit the computer cords one by one, so I couldn't do my assignment at home. I told Auntie Margaret about my school project, and she got on the project since she had a computer. She decided she would do the whole thing. Not only did she do my report, but she ended up finding out Mahalia Jackson was buried in New Orleans, Louisiana. She took me to Mahalia's grave, and I took pictures to go along with my project. Mr. Bowen didn't say we needed to bring in anything extra but our reports. I had more than just a report; I had Mahalia's grave pictures to share with my classmates. I enjoyed the assignment. I learned from the way Auntie Margaret did with my report, it's okay to stand out—not everybody's born to fit in.

The bullying started all over again. Mrs. Belle was very careless, and it got out of control again. I started getting in trouble again. It was the same people that had been messing with me. I guess picking on me was like a trend that never went out of style. I had to tell my granny again, and again, she had to make a trip to the school. I just went through it again, and I accepted that I would be bullied for the rest of my days. It never seemed like it would get better. I went back to those days of crying again when my escape was the library, but I still tried to be proactive. I found myself feeling hopeless, but still I managed to make it. I felt that Carlton was ignoring me at school, so I wrote a horrible letter telling him how upset I was that he didn't want to be bothered.

I gave it to Raina Stove, who I thought was my friend. I wrote the letter through pure anger. I told Raina, "Don't give it to him," since I changed my mind. Raina told me she threw it away, and I believed her. I was standing outside at recess, and Carlton looked at me and said, "You cripple," and he said it loudly.

My God, did I get upset. Raina betrayed me. She gave Carlton my letter, and I was angry and asked her why she gave it to him. I told Raina, "You just don't know what I would do to you."

It all happened so quickly. Raina slapped me in my face. She even pushed me down to the ground. Never had I had a fight in school. I lost the fight and cried loudly. My granny made it to Cali Middle. She caught a ride to come get me. We both got suspended from school, and God knows when I got back to school, I was teased about getting beat up.

I still managed to survive the bullying, I still kept up my behavior, and just like sixth grade, I got rewarded Most Improved, but this time, I ended up getting rewards for my writings in the language arts class.

Seventh grade was a difficult year. Even though Mrs. Darinsky was no longer there, still I kept up my behavior and still I was rewarded Most Improved. I took that as a good thing no matter how difficult it was to get through. At least I passed to the next grade.

# Cali Junior High

*Do not repay anyone evil for evil. Be careful to do what is right in the eyes of everyone. If it is possible, as far as it depends on you, live at peace with everyone. Do not take revenge, my dear, my dear friends, but leave room for God's wrath, for it is written: "It is mine to avenge;*

*I will repay," says the Lord. On the contrary: "If your enemy is hungry, feed him; if he is thirsty, give him something to drink."*

—Romans 12:17–20

My mom ended up moving in 2005, and I would be attending Cali Junior High. It was an all-of-a-sudden move. I wasn't going to be seeing my granny everyday anymore, but I called her and let her know about school. I told my granny I had made new friends where we lived as well as at school. I liked it, but I was nauseous when I got up to go to school every morning. Years of bullying is what I felt made me feel so sick. Even though I no longer lived with my granny, I still would have to go to school with the children that teased me, and I was even in the same class with some of them.

Jorden was in one class with me, and still he would tease me. I remember meeting Sonya Wallis, who had a disability also, and we became friends. I remember telling her about a boy bullying me. I didn't say what his name was until she asked. I said, "Jorden Booker," and she told me he was her uncle.

She said, "Call him a crack baby, and he'll leave you alone."

I was shocked at what Sonya said about her uncle and to find out something like that about him. I didn't call Jorden a crack baby because I knew what it felt like to be called names—hurtful names at that. Even though he teased me about being handicapped and called me so many names—even the fact that he would hit me or push me—it still gave me no reason to give stone for stone. I chose God's way. I was taught to treat others the way you want to be treated, not treat people the way they treat you.

When I would catch the bus to my granny's house, I would get teased, pushed, and shoved; I would have my hair pulled; and I almost got pushed to the floor. Jorden was involved in this act of cruelness. Truth is, there were too many students on that bus anyway.

It was so bad I had to tell my granny about how I would get treated and how children had the audacity to put their hands on me and push me. My granny came to the school, and I told the principal, Mr. Fergus Ellis, about Jorden—how he and some of the other children were pushing me and how he pulled my hair. He said he didn't pull my hair. A high schooler named Nia Talley had pulled my hair. Mr. Ellis told my granny he was not having it, and he dealt with all the children that were involved, and they no longer bothered me. At home, I mostly was online. Keyshia Cole was a new music artist. I loved her music and was doing some research on her when I saw something called Myspace. I remember creating a profile and finding people that I knew, and I added them. I was sent requests by people that knew me—even my friends that I made became my friends online. I liked Myspace, and I loved the fact that I could decorate my page and make it all girly and cute. Never in my mind did I think I would go through anything with my bullies on Myspace. It never crossed my mind.

I was online, and I received a message from Carlton—yes, Carlton, the guy that I kissed. I saw he said, "Hi there," but there was more I didn't know until I read the rest. Carlton said to me, "Hi there, you Handicap Bitch."

I was hurt. I responded back to him and said, "I wasn't a Handicap Bitch when you kissed me," and he had the audacity to deny the kiss.

I should have showed his messages to the cops, but I told my mom and she told his uncle June about him. That was just the beginning when it came down to online bullying, but it got worse. Carlton wasn't the only person who reached out to me from the past, but Raina as well. She wanted to be my friend, and I immediately denied her request, but still I forgave her even though she never apologized. I didn't want to go backward with my life. I forgave both Carlton and Raina, but I didn't want to have anything to do with either of them.

Another time I was on Myspace, I had an image drawn on my page. It was one drawn of me with the curly hairstyle my granny did on me. I was drawn as a stick figure. The sun was shining bright, there was a gun pointing to my head, and they shot me and drew blood flying from my head to the ground.

I sat and looked at this image with tears in my eyes, and I felt like my face would crack open. I wanted to die. I didn't tell anybody. I deleted the image, but it resurfaced again. I didn't know the artist who drew this image on my page. Maybe I did. But whoever they were, they had no heart. I never forgot that image even up until this very day.

It wasn't the end of bullying on my page. There were embarrassing things that were left—profanity was one—but I ended up deleting things off my page where people couldn't write me. There was so much hate thrown my way.

I still remained on Myspace even though I experienced cyberbullying, but when would this hate end? I should've showed that image to somebody, but not me. I suffered within myself. I had to face this the best I could, no matter how hard things got. Through it all, God was watching me, protecting me, and getting me through. I was scared. Late at night I would just cry myself to sleep. I didn't know what would happen next—would they find out where I lived?

# The Bully That Apologized in Junior High

*Forgive and you will be forgiven.*

—Luke 6:37

It's a choice to forgive people when they mistreat you, but I chose to forgive because God forgives us when we do wrong.

I told my uncle Kody about Bryson teasing me in school, and he told Bryson's dad about it. I never knew what all was said between them, but what happened at school shocked me with Bryson. We were outside waiting on the school bus, and it was taking long, so I went and took a seat on the bench. Bryson ended up coming in my direction, and he sat down beside me on the bench, and he said, "Brenaji, I have something to tell you."

I thought it was something negative he had to tell me. Was it a new name he wanted to call me, since he would call me handicap, ugly, and cripple, etc.?

Bryson sounded serious. He said, "Brenaji, I want to apologize." I didn't look him in his face; I was shocked more than anything.

Was I hearing things? Bryson asked me to look him in his eyes, and I did just that. He said he was so sorry for the way he treated me throughout the years. After the apology, Bryson asked me if I accepted his apology, and I told him yes, and he never messed with me again. Even when Bryson saw children teasing me on the bus or at school, he no longer participated. I thank Bryson for not just *saying* sorry, because he was actually sorry and showed it. A burden was lifted off my shoulder. I may have had over ten bullies, but at least, one freed me.

In the end, I stopped riding the bus to my granny's house. My grandpa would drive me to see my granny in the end. I was two years behind in school because I was held back in kindergarten as well as fourth grade. I wasn't the only student behind in school, and I couldn't concentrate like I did before the bullying. I wanted so desperately to be in my right grade. I really felt stupid.

But one day, several students that were behind in school were called to the cafeteria to discuss another option we could take if we wanted to and that was to get in the Options III program. The Options III put students in their right grade, and you would work toward getting a GED. I brought the paperwork home to my mom and told her it was what I wanted to do instead. I was no longer going to Cali Junior High, but I would be going to Cali High School, and my bullies would be still in junior high school. What joy that was for me. Life felt like it couldn't get any better. I got tested to see what level I would be on when I got to Cali High School. I was not at a twelfth, or better yet an eleventh-grade level either, so I had to work—and hard.

# God Gave Me Another Chance

*God does all these things to a person—twice, even three times.*

—Job 33:29

This was another chance God had given me, and I couldn't be happier. I didn't give up even though I wasn't at the right grade level. I ended up being retested, and I made it to Mr. Ed Martin's class. They called it the Exit Room, where students who were actually close to getting their GEDs on a twelfth-grade level are. I didn't take it all that serious, and I found it quite boring at some point just to be in one class up until the bell rang for me to go to ROCEC.

I made friends with a girl, Emmi Dong. She wasn't in the GED program, but she was going to ROCEC too. ROCEC is where I took up a trade in cooking. I actually enjoyed ROCEC. Mrs. Annie Repel was the teacher. She was hilarious. We did all types of stuff—making cakes, king cakes, truffles, etc.

At some point, I felt like I made a mistake by deciding to get a GED. I heard some high schoolers saying the GED students were slow.

I overheard Tranell Quaker, a student who wasn't going for a GED, say loudly, "A GED ain't nothing to get." She seemed like she didn't care if anyone heard her, but I did, and I was going to school for a GED. And as if I that wasn't enough to make me feel down already, at the bus stop a lady that knew I was going to school for a GED said to me she didn't want any of her children to get a GED. She wanted them to all get high school diplomas.

The year came to an end, and still I didn't get my GED. I had one more year left. I never knew, or better yet focused, on the fact that I would or wouldn't get my GED on my last year of high school. I went back to school strong, and I gave it my all. I was back in the Exit Room with Mr. Martin in his class.

There were days when I would struggle, and I found myself standing outside class, talking to him about how I felt like I was a failure. I remember Mr. Martin gave me a coin, and it had the serenity prayer written on it. What stood out to me about it were the words,

"God grant me the serenity to accept what I can't change."

I felt that was my life. I had to accept my past, and maybe—just maybe—if I wasn't bullied, I wouldn't be going to school for a GED. But there was no going backward. I made the decision and had no choice but to go through with it. I was back in the cooking class—this time around with a teacher named Mrs. Brunet Dillard. I noticed I was in the same class with Garla, and I was not comfortable. God knows I told Mrs. Dillard I felt she would make fun of me. It wasn't long that Garla wasn't in class with me. I don't know what happened, because Garla changed her class schedule, and we no longer were in the same class. I noticed this time around that it was different.

I actually did get picked on by Nazi Crawford from another school. She accused me of talking about her, and nobody was talking about her. I didn't respond because I felt she was trying to get a reaction out of me, so I remained proactive.

That year I learned a lot more how to make caramel popcorn, chocolate chip cookies, homemade pizza, you name it. I loved learning about how to fix certain foods and deserts as well because I liked eating.

The class took a test, and why did I tell Ada Jack that I felt Mrs. Dillard didn't like me because I got a B instead of an A for my class grade? Mrs. Dillard was the one that told me that Ada told her what

I said about her, and God knows I knew never to say anything to Ada about how I felt. I didn't even tell Ada I knew what she had done. I just hated drama. Maybe because I was quiet, she probably just wanted me to get in trouble.

Once, when Mrs. Dillard was on duty at break for the week, the whole class left to take a break, but I chose not to. I stayed in class by myself. I heard a familiar voice in the kitchen part of the class. It was Mrs. Kimble. She knew Mrs. Dillard and was looking for her. As I sat in the desk, I began to shake so uncontrollably even the desk shook. I thought I was going to pass out, my nerves had gotten the best of me. I was afraid. I begged God silently to please not let Mrs. Kimble come near me. She didn't come near me; she just left the building. I felt relieved and took a deep breath and exhaled.

Since ROCEC had the cosmetology service, all classes throughout campus would get a chance to get a free service done, and I got picked. My ex-friend Don was the person I got assigned to, and never did she come to do my nails. She did it on purpose, and I just walked out of the class when I saw she was acting like they didn't tell her to do my nails.

I never went to the homecoming dance or the prom, but I wanted to go to my senior year. Why did Breann tell me a story about a girl who went to homecoming and had a horrible experience? Her hair fell down and one of her heels broke, and God knows why I laughed.

I went to the mall, to the Fashion Fair makeup counter, and the makeup artist Carla Cunningham had a hard time matching my foundation—the color was too light, and I looked like an oompa loompa from *The Wizard of Oz* movie. She did a great job on my eyeliner though. Later on that day, my face started to itch, and I broke out from the foundation.

My granny heard about Cali's finest dresses, and my grandpa brought me there. I found an affordable dress that was beautiful, and I got my shoes too.

I was ready when prom day came. All seemed to go well on the day of prom except when I put my shoes on—they seemed too tight. My granny suggested I wear knee-highs, and I did just that. My grandpa drove me to take my pictures at Fabulous Photo Studio. I met up with my friend Emmi Dong and her date, Frank Duvall. I ended up riding with them to Food Is a Must restaurant, and we ate there. Frank told me I had something between my teeth—it was the salad. How embarrassing; that never happened to me before.

I was so glad when we made it to the dance at school. I ended up dancing with one of my friends, Tone McGee. As Tone and I were talking, all a sudden, one foot went before the other one because I had taken my shoes off and kept the knee-highs on, and I slipped before I knew it. So many couples looked my way and laughed, and I laughed too.

For me, it would be a night to remember, and I thought about the story my sister told me; and I felt because I laughed about it, that's why I fell at my first prom. Poor Tone, he didn't even help me up. His mouth was wide open—if a bee would have been in the building, it would've gone in his mouth.

After I fell, the Lil Wayne song "Lollipop" came on, and I danced the night away. I took so many pictures. It was a special moment I will forever cherish. That night at prom, one of the people I saw was none other than Zelda. It was enough that she stared at me every time she saw me in school as though she never saw me before and didn't say a word each time. I did my best to ignore her stares.

Zelda looked at me, and she actually said, "Hey, Brenaji," and I told her *hey* back. I don't know what happened to her after all those years—maybe she didn't dislike me, maybe.

I went home and told my granny about my prom, and we laughed.

Back at school, I talked to Mr. Martin because I still wasn't happy that I wasn't close or made it to get my GED. And before I knew it, I remember him saying I couldn't read. I had dyslexia, and I dealt with it the best way I could. I took it like a champ, and I refused to give up. I might not have gotten my GED in his class, but still, I wasn't giving up. He didn't know my story.

Before I knew it, the time had come when I was no longer going to be in high school. I didn't get my GED, but that didn't mean I couldn't walk with the class. I missed the first graduation rehearsal purposely because I felt it was a waste of time. I hadn't accomplished anything. I had a change of heart and went to the second practice, which made me stand further down the line of graduates since I didn't go to the first practice. I remember walking with the class of 2008, my original class, and it felt good just to walk.

I graduated with a completion certificate, but that wasn't enough. I had to do something, and quickly. It was not long that I made a move from my mom's and back with my granny after high school. I told my granny I wanted to go back to school. I made the decision to go for it. I called California Adult School and enrolled myself to go back to school that August. I kept in mind when I was faced with obstacles about myself as a baby, I was a fighter, and I didn't give up easily even with bullying. I chose to go for a GED, another challenge. Just like the others, I could get through it with the help of God.

# *When Change Knocks, Allow It to Come in Your Life*

*There is a time for everything, and a season for every activity under the heavens.*
—Ecclesiastes 3:1

I enrolled in adult school in 2008. I started taking classes in August just like I would have if I were in regular school. My granny didn't have a car either, so if I really wanted to go to school, I had no choice but to ride transit buses. I was embarrassed riding the bus at first because people would look at me sometimes strangely, making me feel uncomfortable. I liked going to school. I met so many kind people and almost forgot nice people existed. My granny ended up remodeling her house, and I ended up staying with my mom. I walked from where my mom stayed to the school; thank God it was right up in the front. I had to walk. I had no choice.

Somedays I didn't walk alone. I met Maloney Ruiz, who brought her kid as well, and we would walk to school together.

I saw Ariah Lowell. I remembered her because she was bringing her daughter to nursery on the bus. Ariah rode with her cousin Roxy to and from school. I was headed home, and someone screamed out, "Do you want a ride?" It was Ariah with her cousin. I said yes, and that's when a friendship was built.

Ariah was older than me. She had three kids, and she brought her little girl, Maliah, to school as well. I admired her and her story. She was in a bad relationship with her two older children's father and ended up getting together with a man who treated her well. Ariah would look out for me to get me home, and her cousin didn't mind. When we would go to the snowball stand, Ariah's cousin refused to let me pay for my snowball and refused to take money from me when I offered it to her. She said God was going to bless her. I always would thank her. Ariah had a huge heart. She even had her aunt Gerry Cole bring me home. I thanked her as well.

I became friends with an older lady named Stella Marques, and she told me years ago that she and her nineteen-year-old daughter were going to school together, but she got murdered. Mrs. Marques would sit in her truck, and one morning, she motioned her hand for me to go where she was, and she went to the store and bought me a sandwich, chips, as well as a drink. I found it to be too much, and she didn't do this for me one day, but for days. I always would thank her for her kindness.

Mrs. Marques wasn't the only one who would pay for something I ate. A teacher, Mrs. Julia Snyder, would also. Noel West and I were outside talking about math, and neither of us ate, and she walked up to us and gave us tacos she bought. We both thanked her. It wouldn't be the last time Mrs. Snyder bought me anything. She bought me pizza too. I honestly didn't have money, and I didn't tell anyone that either.

My granny gave me money to catch the bus, and sometimes I would have a little change, and I would buy myself a snack out the snack machine, or I would bring a sandwich and some chips.

There were so many people that helped me at adult school.

Some days I would be in doubt. I imagined myself as a grayheaded woman sitting on the bench, seeing youngsters getting their GEDs, but not me. I had to get the thought out of my head. I had to work hard to earn my GED, and besides, I didn't want it handed to me, so I had to work hard and however long it took.

I was sitting in class, and Tranell, the same girl that said a GED was nothing to get, was there—she was going to school to get a GED. I learned you have to be mindful of what you say, or it will come back and haunt you. I don't know if Tranell ever finished school, but she should've thought before she spoke.

Still while attending adult school in 2009, I became interested in learning how to drive. I called EOP driving school and got in and went to the school at night. I refused to let my disability stop me from getting my driver's license. I did the paperwork at school, but not the driving, because a family member said they would teach me how to drive. I passed the paperwork with a 93 percent, and the next step was going to the DMV and getting my driver's permit, and I did. It was not easy, and I didn't pass my first test. It was confusing, but I didn't stop until I got my permit to drive. My granny encouraged me to keep trying, and I did that and prayed. I was glad I had accomplished my goal.

Both Noel and Ariah took their GED test, and both of them passed. I congratulated both of them, but still I wondered when my turn would come. Afterward, Noel and Ariah both were helping other students in class. Noel helped me with my math, and he was able to tell Mrs. Lucy Font, the math teacher, where to put me in math to help me, and I caught on and didn't struggle.

After a while, I ended up quitting. I just grew tired of trying. I just gave up. I moved back in with my granny, and I decided over the summer that I would give adult school another try for my GED. It wasn't easy. I didn't just go to class for the morning class, but I went in the afternoon as well. I was determined to finish what I had started. I was so determined, I bought a GED practice book and practiced at home. I finally reached the point where I was able to finally take the practice GED test, and I didn't do well at first, and then I was assigned to do more work when I struggled.

I didn't like to go back. It made me feel like I would never get through, but I put in hard work until I signed up and paid to take my GED test. I was so nervous. I remember talking to Auntie Helga on the phone, and she told me to bring a bottle of water, and I did just that.

In 2010, my uncle Makhi took me to the main library to take the GED test. In about two weeks, I got a large yellow envelope in the mail. It was my GED results. I broke down and cried after receiving my results. I had failed both science and social studies. I told my granny I wasn't going to retake the test.

My granny said, "Yes, you are."

I dried my teary face. I thought back to what my granny would always say, "You're considered a failure unless you try."

I signed back up again. I prayed and asked God to go in the room before me and take away any negative thoughts of failure. I brought a bottle of water. I found my nerves were bad, and nothing but God directed me to put my wrist underneath cool water in the bathroom sink, and I was calm. I used test-taking tips from Uncle Maine. He told me to read the questions first, and you know, it worked. I remembered so much of the information that was put before me from my days of elementary as well as middle school. I felt confident and felt I had passed.

This time, when the large yellow envelope came through the mail, I had passed. God heard my prayer request, and he delivered. I was proud of myself. I had obtained my GED with God's help. Without him, I wouldn't have been able to do it.

After I got my GED, Auntie Margaret brought me to California Technical Community College. She filled out my financial aid information, and God knows I never knew what I really wanted to be. My major was general studies.

A new chapter began for me in 2011—college it was. Then I got interested in another program in 2013 and stopped going to. I went to CTA, where I took up computer information systems.

Years had passed, and my family members that said they would teach me how to drive never did. It hurt me for years. I waited and cried and prayed. I was online, looking for someone to teach me. I even called EOP driving school, but I couldn't get through. I was told I would get a callback, but I never did. But I wasn't giving up until I got my break. I was going to school at CTA Monday through Thursday, and on Fridays there was no school.

Then the opportunity I had been waiting happened—I found a driving instructor named Mr. Nomad Max (he was an older man). I told my granny, and she wanted me to make sure it was legit. I did my research, and it was.

If I didn't have a driving permit, I wasn't going to be able to drive, Mr. Max informed me. Thank God I did have my permit. I drove with him on Fridays. I drove maybe five times or less than that. I decided I wanted to take my driver's test to get my license. The same family members that said they would teach me how to drive told me that in order to get my driver's license, I was going to have to drive a car, and I didn't have a car. I let it go—not everybody in your family wants to help you. I learned to be independent.

Mr. Max told me to go back to the school (EOP) where I passed my test so that I could drive with them, and I didn't have to worry about using anybody's car. I used the driving school's car to drive. God fixed everything I worried about for me, but on his time, not mine.

The first time I drove at EOP, I was so nervous that I made several mistakes and failed. I cried after I failed. I called my granny and told her. She motivated me to go back and try again, and yes, I passed and became a licensed driver in 2014.

And not only that, I graduated from CTA that same year. I didn't let my disability stop me from doing anything. I tried first, and even if I failed, I would try again and again until I got it. Giving up was not an option. Besides, I was born a fighter. Even back then, I didn't give up when faced with adversity. I still refused to give up. Sometimes I wondered where God was, but he was there the whole step of the way—with me—bringing me through what seemed like a mess, because there was a message that I would one day share with the world.

# Chose to Walk on the Path of Forgiveness

*And Jesus said, "Father, forgive them, for they know not what they do." And they cast lots to divide his great garments.*

—Luke 23:34

Many paths presented themselves to me—two, at least. Unforgiveness and forgiveness. The path of unforgiveness was a path filled with anger, hatred, and holding grudges against others that wronged me. Then there was forgiveness, a path with no anger, hatred, bitterness, but happiness and freedom. God stood beside me as I made my decision. I took one step, then plenty more. Before I knew it, I walked on the path of forgiveness.

But even though I made the decision to forgive, forgiveness itself doesn't erase those painful memories. That's where God comes in. I had to ask him to help me to forgive.

I'm not perfect. I have made mistakes and have done wrong, but I remember God forgives me when I do wrong and when I ask him to forgive me.

I have no regrets about my past; it only made me stronger. It was a test, and no test lasts forever—life itself doesn't either.

This is my testimony. God made me this way for a reason. He allowed me to walk not just for a reason but for several, and for that I am so thankful. I never knew what I wanted to become, but I figured it out: a model, since I loved taking pictures when I was a kid. Not only do I want to be a model, but I also want to be a role model for those that suffer with acceptance from others. I don't want others to look up to me but up to the one that I look up to (God).

I am back in college, furthering my education. I continue walking on this journey. All is forgiven, and my heart has not been hardened, but it has been healed. I walk with love, willingness, strength, faith, and hope from God up above. I am the walking testimony. I stood the test, I gave it my best, and God took care of the rest.

www.ingramcontent.com/pod-product-compliance
Lightning Source LLC
Chambersburg PA
CBHW060413080526
44583CB00012B/549